QUESTIONING HISTORY

The Holocaust

Pat Levy

HODDER
Wayland

an imprint of Hodder Children's Books

© 2003 White-Thomson Publishing Ltd

Produced for Hodder Wayland by
White-Thomson Publishing Ltd
2/3 St Andrew's Place
Lewes BN7 1UP

Other titles in this series:
The African-American Slave Trade
The Causes of World War II
The Cold War
The Western Front

Editor: Cath Senker
Designer: Derek Lee
Consultant: Terry Charman
Picture research: Shelley Noronha and
Cath Senker, Glass Onion Pictures
Proofreader: Philippa Smith

Published in Great Britain in 2003 by Hodder
Wayland, an imprint of Hodder Children's Books

British Library Cataloguing in Publication Data
Levy, Patricia, 1951–

The Holocaust. – (Questioning history)
1. Holocaust, Jewish (1939–1945) – Juvenile
literature
I. Title II. Senker, Cath
940.5'3'18

ISBN 0 7502 4084 9

Printed in Hong Kong

Hodder Children's Books
A division of Hodder Headline Limited
338 Euston Road, London NW1 3BH

Picture acknowledgements:
AKG 6, 7, 10, 12, 13, 14, 16, 17, 18, 21, 24, 26,
34, 35, 39, 41, 43, 51, 55; Camera Press 38, 40,
50, 53, 54, 61 (above); Hodder Wayland Picture
Library 20, 30, 31, (U.S.H.M.N.) 32, (Wiener)
37, 42, (Panstwoe Museum) 48, 60 (above);
Mary Evans 11, 15, 27, 28; Popperfoto *cover, title
page*, 4, 8, 19, 22, 23, 33, 44, 46, 47, 49, 56, 57,
58, 59, 60 (below), 61 (below); Topham 9;
WTPix 52.

The map on p5, produced by The Map Studio, is
based on the map on p233 of *A Historical Atlas of
the Jewish People* (Hutchinson, 1992)

Cover picture: Children peer from behind barbed
wire as they await their release during the
liberation of the Auschwitz concentration camp,
January 1945.

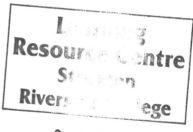

CONTENTS

CHAPTER 1

What Started the Holocaust?

WHAT WAS THE HOLOCAUST?

Between 1933 and 1945 the Nazis murdered millions of Jews as well as minority groups that included gays and disabled people. Jewish populations were forced into ghettos where they were deliberately deprived of the means to stay alive. Many hundreds of thousands were forced on to cattle trucks and transported to death camps. They were starved, beaten or worked to death, shot or gassed to death, in most cases simply because they were Jews.

This was an act of genocide, the deliberate and wholesale slaughter of an entire group of people. To the Nazis, it was the 'Final Solution to the Jewish Question'. From the 1960s this catastrophe, one that cost 6 million Jews their lives, came to be known as the Holocaust. In Hebrew, it was named the Shoah.

BELOW *Child survivors at Auschwitz concentration camp, liberated by Soviet troops in January 1945.*

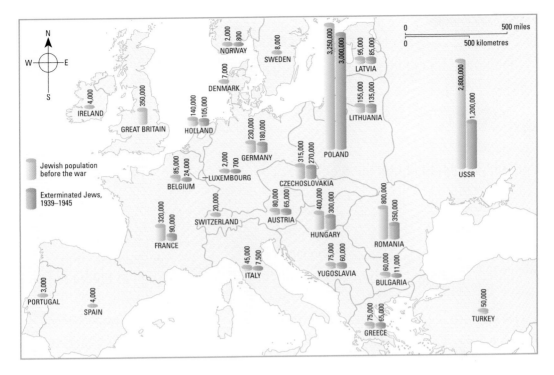

When Did the Holocaust Begin?

The Holocaust may be viewed as beginning with the outbreak of World War II in 1939. Germany conquered much of western Europe and the Jewish population of the whole region fell to the mercy of Nazism. In 1941, after Germany invaded the USSR, special forces from the Nazi SS, called *Einsatzgruppen*, rounded up and murdered Jews and communists in the west of the USSR. Death camps were built in Poland, and Jews were sent there from all over occupied Europe. By the end of the war in 1945, 67 per cent of Europe's Jews had been killed and the Jewish culture of eastern Europe had been virtually destroyed.

Although the Holocaust started with the mass killings in Nazi-occupied Poland, the origins of what happened need to be seen in the context of Jewish history.

ABOVE *This map shows the numbers of Jewish people who were murdered in each region of Europe during the Holocaust.*

? EVENT IN QUESTION

Holocaust Memorial Day

On 27 January 2001, the 56th anniversary of the liberation of the Auschwitz death camp by Soviet soldiers, Britain held its first Holocaust Memorial Day. Of course it is important not to forget the horrors that occurred. The value of Holocaust Memorial Day, however, has been questioned by some people.

It has been argued that it would be better to remember all those who have been victims of genocide, rather than single out the Holocaust. There have been other victims of genocide throughout the world, including many that came after 1945. There were also many victims of Nazism besides Jews.

RIGHT *In 1320 peasants rampaged across France attacking Jewish communities and murdering thousands. Here they are shown besieging the town of Verdun, which sheltered 500 Jews.*

JEWISH HISTORY

The religious culture of Jews, known as Judaism, began in the Mediterranean region in ancient times. Jews lived in the kingdom of Judah, known later as Palestine. By the end of the first century CE there were 5 million Jews living outside Palestine and Jews had also settled in many Christian countries of Europe. After 800 CE the Jews were the only non-Christians in those countries. As a minority group they were open to persecution.

By the eleventh century, the large Jewish communities living across Europe had few rights as citizens. They were restricted to certain trades, such as selling clothes and other goods. Jews lived for the most part in specially marked out areas of each city, known as ghettos. The Church forbade Christians to practise usury – charging interest for lending money – and the job fell to Jewish merchants. Jews became associated with money-lending. They came to be seen as people who exploited the needs of their Christian neighbours.

THE CRUSADES

In 1095 the Pope ordered all Christians to fight a holy war, a crusade, against non-Christians – Muslims and Jews – in the Middle East. The Crusades lasted for about 200 years and during that time Jewish communities were attacked time and time again. By a decree of the Pope, they were forced to wear a mark on their clothing to identify them. The myth emerged that the Jews were murderers of Christian children whose blood they needed for religious rituals.

ANTI-SEMITISM

By the eighteenth century, ideas about the basic equality of all people spread across parts of Europe. In France Jews were made equal citizens. Anti-Semitism, however, remained a strong force and there were several famous cases of persecution against the Jews. In Syria in 1840 a monk and his servant disappeared and, with no evidence at all, the public decided that they had been killed by Jews in order to use their blood in a religious act. Leading members of the Jewish community were arrested, tortured to make them confess and condemned to death.

BELOW Friedrich Nietzsche. His ideas about a race of 'supermen' were misunderstood by the Nazis and used to justify their treatment of those that they considered to be inferior.

? PEOPLE IN QUESTION

Was Nietzsche anti-Semitic?

The philosopher, Friedrich Nietzsche (1844–1900), greatly admired Jewish people and had close friendships with some Jews. In Nietzsche's philosophy, however, it was possible to make out the idea of a 'master race' that had the right to exploit and dominate 'inferior' people.

Nietzsche never intended Jewish people to be identified as an inferior race. But his sister was anti-Semitic and she twisted what he said to make him seem extremely prejudiced. The Nazis accepted this and used Nietzsche to justify their persecution of the Jews. However, nowadays Nietzsche is regarded as a great philosopher who did not hate Jews.

THE DREYFUS CASE

In France, modern anti-Semitism emerged in 1894 when a French army officer named Alfred Dreyfus was imprisoned for selling secrets to the Germans. Despite the later confession of the real spy, Dreyfus was sent back to prison after a second trial. Dreyfus was a Jew and many people believed that Jews were using their new wealth and freedom to harm France. The affair divided the country and brought back to the surface the long tradition of anti-Semitism in Europe.

BELOW *Alfred Dreyfus (1859–1935) spent five years in prison for a crime he did not commit.*

THE GROWTH OF ZIONISM

In late nineteenth-century eastern Europe, there were frequent attacks on Jewish communities and thousands of Jews emigrated to the USA or to Palestine. Small numbers of Jewish people from Russia and eastern Europe had been buying land in Palestine and settling there from the early years of the nineteenth century. In 1897 Theodor Herzl, an Austrian playwright, began a new movement called Zionism. Its aim was to create a safe haven, by open and legal means, for the Jewish people.

The Zionist movement grew in popularity among both Jews and Christians. In 1917, the British government issued the Balfour Declaration, supporting the idea of a Jewish state in Palestine. At the time, the rights of the Arabs already living in Palestine were not considered so important.

ABOVE *Chaim
Weizmann in Palestine,
1918, talking to British
soldiers. Britain ruled
Palestine between 1918
and 1948.*

? PEOPLE IN QUESTION

Chaim Weizmann (1874–1952)

Chaim Weizmann was an industrial chemist and later the first President
of Israel. He became one of the supporters of Zionism and the leader of
the movement in the 1920s. Weizmann saw the increasingly ugly nature
of anti-Semitism that was spreading across Europe. He thought the only
solution was to create a country for the Jews in Palestine.

Yet there were alternatives to Weizmann's ideas. Jews could have
maintained their lifestyle within European society, insisting on their
rights to practise their culture. Alternatively, they could have assimilated
– joined more closely – the Christian society of Europe, abandoning
their language and cultural values. Weizmann rejected these
possibilities. At the turn of the twentieth century, thousands of young
Jewish people followed him into the Zionist movement. Others felt they
had the right to live as Jews in Europe and still others hoped to
integrate more fully into European culture.

WHY GERMANY?

In Germany, Jewish people were able to take an active part in social and economic life but they were banned from holding high government office. After losing the First World War, however, Germany suffered terrible economic hardship. Although Jewish soldiers had fought in the war, Jews became a scapegoat for Germany's failure. Some people accused them of having avoided combat duty and of making money out of the war. At the same time, Germany's new democratic government gave all citizens full and equal rights under the law.

THE NATIONAL SOCIALISTS

While Germany recovered from defeat in war, a new party called the NSDAP (National Socialist Party of German Workers) was formed. Young Adolf Hitler was a leading member. By the early 1920s, this party was accusing Jews of contributing to Germany's downfall. Anti-Jewish feeling grew, with hundreds of anti-Semitic organizations founded across the country. In 1920, the fake Russian document *Protocols of the Elders of Zion* was

BELOW *Following the New York Stock exchange crash of 1929 the German economy collapsed and 3 million people were out of work by the end of 1930. These men in Berlin are studying the newspaper looking for work.*

LEFT *This German children's book published in 1935 shows a rich Jew trying to persuade a blonde Aryan girl to come with him by offering her a string of pearls.*

published in Germany for the first time and widely read. Its publishers claimed it was a genuine document written by Jewish leaders who were planning the overthrow of the Western world.

Meanwhile, the German government became increasingly unstable as economic conditions grew worse. In 1928 the National Socialists won only 800,000 votes. They gained some 14 million votes in the elections of July 1932, almost one-third of the total. The National Socialists, or Nazis as they were now called, were especially successful in attracting votes from middle-class groups who felt threatened by economic chaos. They played down their anti-Semitic beliefs at this stage. No one party in parliament had a clear majority and the parliamentary system looked likely to collapse. In this situation, Hitler, now leader of the Nazis, was invited to become the country's leader.

? PEOPLE IN QUESTION

No Hitler, no Holocaust?

Historians have viewed Hitler's anti-Semitism in different ways. One theory is that he deliberately exploited a prejudice that already existed in order to gain power. Other historians see Hitler's anti-Semitism as the product of a disturbed early life. As a poor, out-of-work artist in Austria he saw wealthy Jews and resented them. Another theory places anti-Semitism at the heart of Nazi ideas. In his writings Hitler describes Jews as a disease or as 'subhumans' (less than humans) bent on destroying Western civilization.

Most historians agree that Hitler was self-absorbed, paranoid and genuinely anti-Semitic. Whether or not he set out at an early stage to exterminate European Jews, according to the historian Milton Himmelfarb, Hitler was certainly the driving force behind the Holocaust. Without him the horror might never have happened.

ABOVE *Germans survey some of the damage left after the Night of Broken Glass.*

NAZIS IN POWER

The war against the Jews began when the Nazis got into power in Germany. In 1935 the Nuremberg Laws stripped Germany's 525,000 Jews of many of their basic rights as citizens. Jews were barred from marrying other Germans and banned from many jobs and professions. Jewish people began to emigrate. On 6 November 1938 a young Jew, whose parents had been deported from Germany, assassinated a German diplomat in France.

This was the excuse the Nazis needed to attack Jewish homes and businesses in Germany. Synagogues were burned to the ground and Jewish shops were looted. Nearly a hundred Jews were killed and 26,000 were arrested and taken away to work camps. The event became known as *Kristallnacht* (Night of Broken Glass). Over the following days, the Nazi government blamed the Jews for the chaos and demanded that the Jews pay compensation to the state for the damage done. Jews were barred from schools, from public places and from the few jobs still left open to them. Over the next few years, all those who were able to left the country.

JEWISH REFUGEES

Faced with the plight of Jewish refugees from Germany, over thirty foreign governments met at Evian, France in July 1938. Instead of condemning the German actions, they sent a message to the German government that they would not interfere with Germany's internal policies. Of all the countries which sent representatives to the conference, only Holland and Denmark agreed to increase the number of refugees that they would allow into their country. After *Kristallnacht* the British government agreed to take in 10,000 unaccompanied Jewish children from Germany.

? WHAT IF...

other European powers had acted sooner?

In 1938 and early 1939, the countries that might have stopped Hitler from invading other lands were unprepared for war. Britain hoped that war could be avoided, while the USA had little interest in becoming involved in a European conflict. Britain was not interested in allying with the communist USSR against Germany. Later, these countries did form an alliance against Germany. Some historians say that war, and the Holocaust, could have been avoided if they had acted sooner.

War Looms

In March 1938 Germany had annexed (taken control of) Austria, with the support of the Austrian people, bringing another 180,000 Jewish people under Nazi control. In September Hitler demanded that Sudetenland, part of Czechoslovakia, be handed over to Germany. It was obvious that war was looming in Europe but the British Prime Minister, Neville Chamberlain, went to Germany to meet Hitler. He brought back a peace agreement that he hoped would avoid war.

BELOW *March 1938: Hitler arrives in Vienna to celebrate the annexation of Austria.*

LEBENSRAUM

Hitler, meanwhile, was developing another thread in the Nazi outlook, the idea of *Lebensraum* – German for 'living space'. This meant taking over other lands to provide room for the 'Aryan race' – the blue-eyed German people – to flourish. To the east of Germany lay Poland and the Soviet Union where Slavs lived. Nazism regarded Slavs as an inferior race and Hitler now set about acquiring their land.

WORLD WAR II BEGINS

In September 1939 Germany invaded Poland and, the following year, Belgium, Holland, Denmark, Norway, Luxembourg and France. In 1941 Greece, Yugoslavia and the USSR were invaded.

BELOW *As German troops made their way into Poland, Jewish families were driven from their homes and their possessions were destroyed, as seen here.*

By then Germany had most of Europe's Jewish population, about 5 million people, at its mercy. Jews who had earlier fled Germany to other parts of Europe now found themselves trapped once more. Germany was opposed only by Britain in the west and the USSR in the east. But the main aim of those countries was not to save Jews from Nazism. World War II was a battle between strong nations for power.

As he set about taking control of most of Europe, Hitler determined to deal with European Jewry as a whole. Jews were forbidden to leave Poland and the other countries occupied by Germany. One plan was to make a massive camp in Poland where all Jews could be held; this plan would lead to the Holocaust.

? WHAT IF...

Jewish people had been allowed to emigrate?

If Germany had been content to drive Jewish people out of the lands they controlled, where could they have gone? The traditional homeland of the Jewish people was Judah (later Palestine) in the Middle East. In 1939 Palestine was governed by the British government, which refused throughout the war to allow refugees to enter. The British feared an Arab uprising in support of Germany, leading to the loss of British control in the Middle East.

The USA and Britain, two countries not overrun by Germany, allowed in only a strict quota of refugees. The USSR was open to Jewish refugees but they got little comfort there; they were simply transported further east, along with thousands of people from other Russian minority groups. Japan, however, took in some refugees. If the countries not occupied by the Nazis had offered shelter to all the Jewish refugees, how many more might have been saved?

BELOW *This picture from a Jewish publication of 1933 promotes Jewish emigration to Palestine.*

Chanukah-Tage im jüdischen Dorf

Palästina
Bild-Beilage
der Jüdischen Rundschau
Berlin W 15, Meinekestraße 1

Nr. 5 99 vom 12. Dezember 195

CHAPTER 2

What Happened in the Holocaust?

THE GHETTOS

In autumn 1941, many Jews in Germany and the German-occupied countries of Austria and Czechoslovakia were deported to Poland. They were forced to live in ghettos, which were set up in major towns there. These were enclosed by walls and guarded at night. Jewish Councils, made up of elders who were community leaders, were responsible for organizing the day-to-day affairs of the ghettos. Laws were enforced by the Jewish police.

BELOW *The ghetto of the city of Lublin in eastern Poland. The Germans established Majdanek concentration and extermination camp nearby. Thousands of people from this ghetto died there.*

Whole families lived in single rooms and few people without a secret store of wealth survived the harsh winter and gruelling labour. They had to work in arms factories and on building projects, constructing roads and fortifications. As adults died, children were left to beg in the streets. Diseases such as typhoid broke out in the unhealthy conditions. Anyone leaving the ghetto or anyone bringing aid to those inside was shot.

The people working for the Jewish Councils faced a very difficult task. Their job was to collect taxes, to organize work parties, and later to choose who would join the transports to the death camps. So the Jewish Councils became part of the Nazi machinery of death. Historians have shown that the Jewish Councils in the many ghettos of eastern Europe did not always behave in the same way. Some refused to do the Nazis' work, while others co-operated to the full in the hope of saving at least some lives. Other ghettos had no Jewish Councils and transports to the death camps were organized by the Nazis themselves.

Mordechai Chaim Rumkovski: hero or villain?

Chaim Rumkovski (1877–1944) was the Jewish Council leader in the ghetto of Lodz, Poland. He organized the rounding up of all the ghetto's children, and the weak, sick and elderly, knowing that they were going to be gassed. He ran the ghetto as a dictator and had ultimate power over the life and death of all its inmates. Lodz was the last ghetto to be cleared in August 1944 by having its remaining population sent to the death camps.

Three days short of liberating Lodz, Soviet troops halted their advance into German-occupied Poland for the winter. By the time they reached Lodz some months later, the ghetto had been cleared by the Nazis. If the Soviets had arrived before the winter, Rumkovski's plan to be useful to the Germans in order to save the inmates could have paid off. Some 69,000 Jews from the Lodz ghetto might have survived. Would this have made Chaim Rumkovski a Jewish hero rather than a hate figure?

ABOVE *The Jewish police in the Warsaw ghetto, lined up ready for inspection. They had to round up people to send to the death camps.*

THE DEATH SQUADS

As German troops pushed into eastern Europe in 1941, the Nazi *Einsatzgruppen* were ordered to round up Jews, gypsies and communists, and murder them. In Byelorussia, Ukraine, Latvia and Lithuania in 1941, 40,000 German troops – including ordinary German policemen as well as soldiers and local people sympathetic to the Nazis – killed nearly half a million Jews.

The Jews were machine-gunned, individually shot or beaten to death. Eyewitness accounts describe people being forced to dig mass graves and then take off their clothes and climb down into them to be shot. In the later stages victims had to crawl across the bodies of those shot before them in order to be in the right place to die.

Heinrich Himmler, the head of the SS, visited Minsk in August 1941 to observe the *Einsatzgruppen* at work. He demanded that an alternative be found so as to make the work more efficient and less distressing for the soldiers that carried it out. There were so many Jewish people that ghettos were specially built to contain them until they could be murdered.

After Himmler's visit to Minsk in 1941, the plan for the 'Final Solution to the Jewish Problem' went into operation. Mobile gas vans were put into operation in Serbia, Latvia and Poland. Fixed killing sites were set up in Poland at Belzec, Sobibor, Chelmo, Madjanek and Treblinka. At Auschwitz in Poland both a death camp and a large work camp were built.

BELOW *Otto Ohlendorf. At his trial at Nuremburg his defence was that a soldier was obliged to obey orders given by his superior.*

? PEOPLE IN QUESTION

Otto Ohlendorf: just doing his job?

Otto Ohlendorf (1907–1951) was head of *Einsatzgruppe D*, one of the special murder units that operated in the Crimea and southern Ukraine. After the war he was tried and executed as a war criminal. To his fellow officers and the men who served under him, however, he was a fair and humane commander. He refused to allow anyone who had no stomach for murder to take part in the executions and had them transferred to easier jobs. His colleagues saw him as genuinely committed to the ideal of creating an Aryan paradise in the Soviet Union. He believed that Jewish people were so evil that the only choice for the Nazis was to kill every single one. Ohlendorf was personally responsible for the callous murder of 90,000 Jewish innocents and other victims, rounding up all the Jews that he could find and having them massacred.

19

ABOVE *Adolf
Hitler developed
his beliefs about
the Jews as a young
man growing up in
Austria. The Nazi Party's
extreme anti-Semitism
was demonstrated by
the policy adopted at
the Wannsee Conference.*

THE WANNSEE CONFERENCE

By the beginning of 1942, the Nazis had invaded the Soviet Union and now had vast numbers of Jews under their control. In January, the Nazi government held a meeting at Wannsee in the suburbs of Berlin, Germany, where a new policy was put before the delegates. Europe was to be combed from one end to the other and all Jews were to be transported to Poland. The fittest would be put to work until they died from exhaustion. The unfit would be killed. Any who survived would be murdered since they would represent the strongest of the Jews and might one day produce children who would take their revenge.

THE STRAIGHT OR THE TWISTED PATH?

Some historians, such as Lucy Dawidowicz in *The War against the Jews*, argue that the whole Holocaust process that began at Wannsee had been intended much earlier and was a deliberately planned policy. This is known as the intentionalist interpretation. Other historians, such as Uwe Adam, think that the idea of genocide gradually occurred to the Nazi government as it gained more and more control over Europe. They adopted the policy as the situation developed. This is known as the functionalist explanation.

Intentionalist historians believe in 'the straight path' – that the Holocaust was driven by Hitler's personal hatred of the Jews.

They believe that Hitler's motives in starting World War II were to gain land and materials, and to eliminate the Jews of Europe. Intentionalist historians support this idea by referring to Hitler's many speeches and writings, from as early as 1919, in which he expressed his feelings and intentions towards the Jews. Functionalist historians prefer 'the twisted path'. They believe that Hitler was incapable of such long-term planning and that the idea of the Final Solution only came to him sometime late in 1941 as the events of the war unfolded.

BELOW *June 1941: German tanks move over the Polish border into Soviet-occupied territory.*

? EVENT IN QUESTION

*O*peration *B*arbarossa: intentionalist or functionalist?

Operation Barbarossa, the code-name for the Nazi invasion of the Soviet Union that began in June 1941, illustrates the controversy between historians over the nature of the Holocaust. Until this time German Jews had been allowed to emigrate after paying large sums of money. Polish Jews and the remaining German Jews had been crowded into ghettos in Poland and forced to do work for the war effort. This supports the functionalist argument. The decision to massacre all Soviet Jews, on the other hand, had probably already been taken before Operation Barbarossa got under way, and this would support the intentionalist interpretation. If, though, it had always been Hitler's intention to kill all of Europe's Jews, why would he have allowed any of them to emigrate?

THE DEATH CAMPS

In 1941 six death camps were set up in Nazi-occupied Poland. Jews were taken straight to gas chambers and killed. Some 225,000 people died at Chelmno in the gas vans, 250,000 at Sobibor, 600,000 at Belzec and 974,000 at Treblinka. At Majdanek 200,000 people died. Auschwitz was different. People worked at this huge camp producing goods for the Nazi war effort. There were barracks, factories, medical centres, huts, gas chambers and crematoria. Over a million people probably died at Auschwitz camp.

BELOW *A German concentration camp. Political prisoners are put to work while German criminals act as supervisors.*

At Auschwitz work camp, and other work camps in Germany, Austria, Yugoslavia and France, people had their possessions confiscated, were crowded into barracks, tattooed, and given inadequate uniforms and food. They were forced to work until exhausted, they were beaten and tortured and often murdered.

Each of the five purpose-built death camps had only about 90 to 120 staff. Most of the work was done by Jewish work groups. Jewish inmates cleared away the corpses, sorted belongings and kept order among the Jews waiting for their deaths. After victims were gassed, any gold teeth were extracted. Their hair was also removed because it could be sold. The bodies were hauled off, still warm, to crematoria or huge pyres for burning bodies.

THERESIENSTADT AND BERGEN-BELSEN

There were two camps that had slightly different purposes. Theresienstadt (see picture) in Bohemia-Moravia, was set up as a model camp. Wealthy Jewish people paid for the 'privilege' of being sent there. A Nazi propaganda film was produced showing healthy-looking inmates with gardens and happy children. In reality, the camp was a holding station from which people were sent to the death camps.

Another camp, built at Bergen-Belsen in Germany in 1943, held Jews who were to be handed over in exchange for German prisoners of war. Towards the end of the war, however, the camp took in the survivors from camps in Poland and many thousands died there from typhoid or starvation.

? PEOPLE IN QUESTION

Rudolf Höss: kindly family man and callous killer?

Rudolf Höss (1900–1947) was the commandant of Auschwitz death camp from July 1941 to late 1943. He and his family lived in a house beside the camp, screened off from the inmates. In his autobiography, written while awaiting trial after the war, he describes his happy family life as well as his feelings while administering the camp.

Höss says he was kind to the inmates who worked for him in his house and tried to run the camp as efficiently as he could, preventing guards from stealing Jewish possessions. He describes his great pity for the women he watched carrying their children into the gas chambers. Survivors from the camp, on the other hand, portray him as cruel and ruthless. Could someone have been a kind family man while also administering mass murder?

ABOVE *A Nazi propaganda shot to show good conditions at Theresienstadt camp.*

ZYGMUNT E

ABOVE *A group of Jews being deported from the ghetto of Lodz in central Poland in March 1940.*

LIQUIDATING THE GHETTOS

The Jewish Councils in the ghettos of eastern Europe were ordered to provide daily quotas of Jews for transportation. As the ghettos emptied, more Jews from occupied Europe arrived to take the places of those being transported. The various ghettos responded to this in many different ways.

In Kovno in 1941 the Jewish Councils were given 5,000 cards to distribute to skilled workers. Once they had been issued it became clear that the 25,000 Jews without these *Lebensscheine* (life permits) were to be killed. Panic set in and mobs attacked the Jewish Councils' offices stealing any cards they could find.

? WHAT IF...

the ghettos had resisted?

The Jewish writer, Hannah Arendt, has said that if the ghetto Jews had been less organized and had complied less with the Nazi orders to provide people for the transports and work details, then many more might have survived. Others have wondered why the ghetto Jews did not resist their murderers more. In fact there were uprisings in at least twenty ghettos, including a major one in Warsaw. The people that led these revolts and took part in them showed tremendous courage in the face of the overwhelming force of the Nazis.

Whether the rebellions had any effect on the survival rate of the Jewish people is not clear. It is open to debate whether more widespread resistance would have slowed down the machinery of death. Would more resistance have saved Jews, or just made their inevitable deaths come faster?

The next morning the whole community was lined up in the public square. Those who had got hold of the cards were separated out and the others kept waiting for transport out of the ghetto. In the following weeks the sick and the weak, as well as many women and children, were taken away and killed. Neither co-operation nor resistance could have helped them.

In Vilna, similar passes were issued and many people without them found hiding places under floorboards, in attics and in secret rooms. The Jewish police in Vilna were given the choice of either finding those in hiding or being sent to their own deaths along with their families.

CHAPTER 3

Who Knew about the Holocaust?

HOW MUCH DID ORDINARY GERMANS KNOW OR CARE?

There is evidence to show that in the early history of the Nazi attacks on Jews in the 1930s very few people in Germany actively hated Jews. By 1935, though, people were taking part in demonstrations against Jewish businesses, and Nazi party members were instructed not to do business with Jews. Few Germans could have been in any doubt about the anti-Semitic nature of their government. In November 1938, some 30,000 Jews were imprisoned in concentration camps in Germany. This was never reported in the press although many people knew that Jews were being rounded up.

By 1939, while many people did not agree with public attacks on Jews, few people spoke up against anti-Semitism. Many opponents of Nazism had been imprisoned. Also, people were

BELOW *Germany, April 1933. A group of civilians and Hitler's party militia warn passers-by not to buy goods from Jewish shopkeepers.*

The case of the mixed marriages

In 1939, 30,000 'Aryans', mostly women, were married to German Jews. The Nazis hesitated in removing these Jewish partners because they were married to Aryan Germans. Yet they must have seemed the worst kind of Jews, 'spoiling' the Aryan population with their Jewish blood. In February 1943 in Berlin, 2,000 of these Jewish husbands were arrested and the action brought about the only public protest against the treatment of Jews. Their wives demonstrated on the steps of the Gestapo headquarters, despite the constant threats by the authorities to shoot them. After a week there were 6,000 people demonstrating.

The men were released and most of them survived the war, protected by their Christian families. This raises many questions which historians still debate. Were they released because the Nazis feared a public reaction? Does this event show that if more ordinary Germans discovered that people they knew were being murdered they, like the families of those Jewish men, might have tried to stop it? Or did the event have little significance to the war on Jews in general because it was just a few Germans looking after their own families?

ABOVE *This Jewish man and 'Aryan' woman in Germany, 1935, are forced to wear placards. The woman's reads 'I am the greatest swine and only let Jews in'. The man's says 'As a young Jew I only take German girls into my room.'*

frightened of the consequences of resisting the Nazis and many disliked or were indifferent towards Jews. It is not clear to what extent ordinary German citizens knew, after 1941, that the tens of thousands of German Jews being deported to the east were being murdered.

In national newspapers in 1938, Joseph Goebbels, the head of the Propaganda Ministry, said the aim of the Nazi Party was to make the Jews leave Germany. However, underground (secret) groups who opposed Hitler's regime were reporting by 1939 that the Nazis were intent on genocide.

After 1939, it was said in German newspapers that Jewish people were harming Germany's war effort. Films like *The Eternal Jew* and *Jud Süss*, both released in 1940, portrayed Jews as criminals and perverts, intent on destroying the Aryan way of life and preying on good Aryan women. Over 20 million Germans watched *Jud Süss*. Newspapers never mentioned details of 'The Final Solution', but did talk about a war to kill all the Jews. By 1942, Nazi propaganda had convinced many German citizens that the war had actually been started by Jews.

RIGHT *A poster advertising the film* The Eternal Jew.

Historians disagree about whether the German population as a whole supported the genocide or even knew about it. In *Hitler's Willing Executioners*, Daniel Goldhagen claims that not only was knowledge of genocide widespread but that ordinary German people willingly took part in it. Many other historians, such as Ian Kershaw, have concluded that most Germans were ignorant of the extent of the genocide. They were more concerned with coping with the war situation.

It seems clear that the Nazi regime went to great lengths to keep the death camps a secret from the Allies and the German people. Theresienstadt concentration camp was portrayed as the typical camp in propaganda films and in newspapers. Conditions there were not as terrible as in most camps. The real death camps, such as Auschwitz, were never mentioned in the press.

On the other hand, it was public knowledge that most of Germany's Jews were no longer in the country. Many returning policemen (see panel) would have told their families and friends about the massacres in eastern Europe. Nazi propaganda was successful in convincing many Germans that there was a 'Jewish Question' that needed to be dealt with.

?   EVENT IN QUESTION

Were Germans willing executioners?

In 1942 the members of Police Battalion 101, a company of ordinary Hamburg policemen, were sent to clear the ghetto of Josefow, a small town in Poland. The troops were told what their job was and anyone who didn't want to take part was given the opportunity to leave. A few did. The rest went into the ghetto, murdered the very young and the old in the streets, and herded the rest into trucks which took them to a nearby wood. There each policeman selected a Jew to shoot.

Goldhagen points out that these ordinary men, not fanatical Nazis, dutifully murdered innocents. Other historians such as Yehudah Bauer have taken issue with Goldhagen's interpretation of this event. They point out that very early in Hitler's regime all those who weren't anti-Semitic had been forced out of the police force. In addition, the fact that these ordinary men did this job does not mean that every other German would have done the same.

How Much Did the Jews Know?

There is much evidence that the Nazis attempted to keep Jews ignorant of their intended fate. Those being deported to the east were told to carry supplies for their new life. Jews being taken to the death camps were often issued with postcards to write reassurances to their relatives. These were posted after their deaths. At the death camps themselves, fake signs on the unloading platforms gave the impression to Jews that they had arrived at a normal railway station. Signs around the gas chambers said that they were shower rooms.

BELOW *A postcard from a child, deported to the east, to her father.*

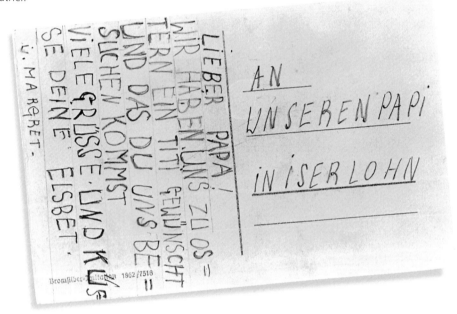

Back in the ghettos, it must have been hard to imagine that the Germans intended to kill every Jewish person in Europe. Many must have hoped that if they obeyed orders, worked hard and made sacrifices, then they might stay alive until the war was over. But by 1943, after the massacres in eastern Europe and the daily demands for more people for transportation, few Jews could have been deceived about what had happened to their friends and neighbours. In addition, a handful of escaped deportees brought the truth back to the ghettos. By this time no one in the ghettos had any illusions about their fate and it was in this year that armed resistance began.

How much did they know in Brest?

The story told by a survivor, Michael Omlimsky, throws a little light on how much the Jews knew about the Nazi plans early in the war. In 1941 he was sent to the ghetto of Brest in the Ukraine. About 17,000 Jews lived there. Soon after he arrived, the Germans chose to murder all the able-bodied young men, to make the ghetto weaker and less able to resist.

Michael, along with a friend, somehow missed the round-up of young men. Michael and his friend ran after the trucks, calling to be let on. They knew so little about what the Germans intended that they thought the other men were being taken to a factory or work camp. The German guards waved them away and Michael survived the war. This indicates that the Jews of Brest had no idea what was to happen to them. Later in the war, though, when news of what was happening reached the ghettos, would Michael have run after the trucks quite so willingly?

BELOW *The ovens in the death camps needed the body fat of the victim to work. But after a time in the camps the bodies were so thin that the ovens failed to work because there was no fat to burn.*

31

HOW MUCH DID THE ALLIES KNOW?

Despite attempts to keep the death camps secret, news of the murders in Poland and the Soviet Union began to be known in 1942, chiefly through the Polish underground resistance. These brave people fought an underground battle against the German occupation of Poland. Men such as Jan Karski travelled widely across the country collecting information on atrocities against the Jews and reporting back to the Polish government in exile in Britain. Throughout the war, the Catholic Church maintained diplomatic relations with Nazi Germany and it was the Church in Bratislava, in the Nazi puppet state of Slovakia, that informed the Pope that the deportations of thousands of Jewish people meant certain death for them.

RIGHT *A Jewish partisan group from Kovno in Lithuania. They hid and lived in the woods and attacked German positions whenever they could.*

In August 1942, a Jewish representative in Switzerland sent messages to the US and British governments saying that an operation had begun to murder all the Jews in countries occupied by Germany. The message even specified that a chemical called Zyklon B would be used to carry out the killings. In a press conference in summer 1942, the British minister for information, Brendan Bracken, denounced 'the beginnings of the wholesale extermination of the Jews'.

With the increasing flow of reports to the Allies, the events unfolding in Nazi-occupied Europe could no longer be denied. In December 1942, the Allies publicly declared that the Germans intended to exterminate the Jews. It wasn't until 1944 that four men escaped from Auschwitz and returned to Hungary with the first detailed accounts of the gas chambers.

? EVENT IN QUESTION

Liberating Buchenwald

'You can't understand it even when you've seen it,' wrote a journalist who was with the Allied troops who liberated Buchenwald concentration camp in April 1945. Soldiers in the American forces declared their inability to understand what they were looking at. Yet as early as 1942, newspapers and governments had confirmed that the Holocaust was happening. How could people have both known about the Holocaust and yet been unable to believe it?

One explanation is that while the information was accepted, neither governments nor newspapers could believe the scope of the tragedy. Others have pointed out that in the USA in 1942, people saw Japan rather than Germany as their real enemy. Yehuda Bauer, an Israeli Jewish historian, mentions a survey of July 1944 in which 44 per cent of Americans saw Jews as a threat and only 6 per cent saw Germans as a threat. Another possibility is that there had never before been an attempt to exterminate an entire race. People weren't able to take in the information and so denied the reality, even when standing in the camp looking at the bodies.

ABOVE *Allied observers – US Congressmen and British Members of Parliament– looking at the scene at Buchenwald after the camp had been liberated.*

33

CHAPTER 4

Could the Holocaust have been Prevented?

COULD THE GERMAN PEOPLE HAVE STOPPED THE HOLOCAUST?

Once Nazism was well established, it was not easy to oppose Hitler. The death penalty was imposed on anyone who tried to 'undermine the will to fight' or anyone who attempted to make a profit from the war. These laws were vague enough to cover a range of activities. Anyone helping Jews or hiding them or even criticizing government policy could be shot or sent to a concentration camp. Despite these restrictions, several hundred Jews survived in Berlin alone, hidden by friends or neighbours.

BELOW *Dietrich Bonhoeffer, a Protestant churchman who opposed the Nazi regime. He was imprisoned in 1943 and executed in April 1945.*

The Christian Churches might have been expected to show some sympathy for the plight of the Jews. However, with a few exceptions, Christians remained neutral or supported the Nazi Party. Some priests helped and defended Jews where they could but the Churches supported the Nazis' opposition to communism. Many of Germany's intellectuals went into exile. Some who remained willingly took over Jewish posts in universities and defended the racist theories.

The way the German people could have prevented the Holocaust was by not voting in large numbers for the Nazi Party in the first place. However, some historians argue that even though the Nazis were associated with attacks on the Jews, they did not gain support because people wanted to see Jews killed. It was only once the Nazis gained power that they seriously put their anti-Semitism into action.

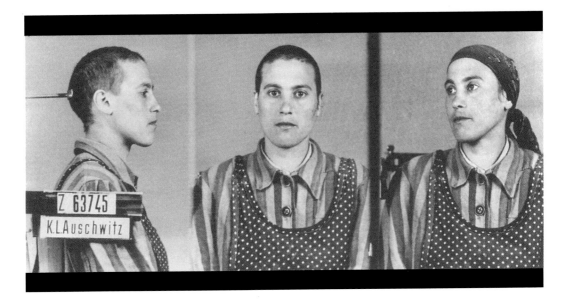

WHAT DID THE JEWS DO?

Many Jews did take what action they could to save themselves. Half of Germany's Jewish population had emigrated by 1939. Any Jews who were able to escape from Nazi-occupied countries did so. Jews outside occupied Europe negotiated with their governments to take more refugees, demanded action from the Allies, collected information and sent money to the ghettos. Some Jews escaped from the ghettos into the woods of eastern Europe and formed partisan groups to save Jews.

ABOVE *A gypsy photographed at Auschwitz death camp. As well as Jews, gypsies, gays and disabled people were murdered by the Nazis.*

? WHAT IF...

Germans had come to the defence of the Jews?

It is difficult to know what might have happened if, in the early days of Hitler's government, Germans had stood up against the uniformed thugs who were attacking the Jews. Hitler, as seen, hesitated to deport Jewish husbands of Christian women (see page 27). In 1941 Hitler officially stopped the programme of 'euthanasia', or mercy killing, through which 70,000 disabled and mentally ill patients had been murdered, because of public protest. Perhaps a protest would at least have saved Germany's Jews temporarily. It is difficult to see how the Holocaust could have been prevented without bringing down Hitler's government and there was certainly not the will to do that.

RESISTANCE OR BETRAYAL?

Once the borders of German-occupied Europe were closed, Jews faced a dilemma. One example of this dilemma happened in 1943 in the ghetto of Vilna in Lithuania. A group of young people obtained weapons and escaped to the forests of Narotch outside the city to join the partisans hiding there. They were stopped by the Germans outside the city and some of them were captured. In return, the Germans killed every member of their families and the leaders of their work groups who had not reported them missing. To those who escaped it may have seemed an act of resistance, but to those who were left behind it was a betrayal.

THE ROLE OF THE PARTISAN GROUPS IN POLAND

Two problems facing the Jews who wished to fight were a lack of weapons and the indifference of partisan groups operating in Poland. The Polish ghetto historian, Emmanuel Ringelbaum, writing during his years in the Warsaw ghetto, concluded that many Poles had helped and hidden Jews, especially in Warsaw. But not enough was done. The Polish resistance wanted to prevent any uprisings in defence of the Jews because they wanted to wait until they could be sure of defeating the Germans.

If the Poles had taken the Jews seriously and given them weapons and help, perhaps some Jews would have escaped. Certainly no more would have died since all were massacred anyway. The Polish underground knew about the deportations. They could have damaged the rail lines and slowed down the killings, maybe saving some lives. However, in their defence, the harshness of the Nazi regime did make it hard for non-Jewish Poles to help the Jews.

WHAT DID THE REST OF EUROPE DO?

Some countries, such as Romania and Croatia, enthusiastically introduced anti-Semitic laws. They put their Jewish populations into ghettos and provided transportation to the east. By 1942 Jews were being sent to Poland from France, Holland, Belgium and Greece, even though news of mass murder was becoming known by then. Organized attempts at rescue only began later in the war.

The help that Jews did receive in Europe was mostly from individuals rather than governments or official organizations such as churches. The only demonstration in Europe against the deportations took place in Holland in February 1941. Individuals there sheltered 20,000 Jews. In parts of France an underground rescue system developed. Hundreds of Jews were helped into neutral Spain where they were relatively safe. In Denmark almost every one of the country's 8,000 Jews was ferried away to the safety of Sweden. Half of Norway's Jews were helped to safety.

BELOW *Jewish partisans from the Vilna ghetto in Lithuania. Abba Kovnr (third from right) was their leader. He survived the war.*

ABOVE *If the Allies had bombed the railway lines to Birkenau (shown here) and Auschwitz it might have delayed the deaths of many thousands of people.*

LACK OF PROTECTION

In Italy anti-Semitic laws meant that Jews were treated harshly, but none were deported until Germany invaded Italy in 1943. With the exception of Italy and Denmark, no government officially protected its Jews. In Hungary, after some initial deportations, the Jews were protected by the state, until Germany invaded in 1944. Then large-scale deportations began. In Bulgaria popular protest stopped the deportations.

WHY DIDN'T THE ALLIES HELP?

Beyond Europe there was much that could have been done to help the Jews. Troop ships carried US soldiers to Britain. They might have collected refugees from fascist but neutral Spain and brought them to safety in the USA. The British government could have allowed Jews to emigrate to Palestine, but didn't because it needed Arab support and oil supplies for the war.

In 1944 the Roosevelt government in the USA established a War Relief Board that dispatched food parcels and supported rescue attempts in Europe. The USA warned the Nazis that it would take action if attacks on Jews continued. But by then most of the killing had been done. Historians do not agree on the reasons for the lack of active help on the part of the Allies. There was a war on and the military need to defeat Germany was regarded as the first priority. That is understandable, but it also possible that anti-Semitic attitudes played a part in the failure to help the Jews.

COULD THE ALLIES HAVE DISRUPTED THE KILLING MACHINE?

By November 1943 the Allies knew the locations of some of the death camps and had control of some airfields in Italy. They could have bombed the gas chambers and perhaps in the chaos some inmates might have escaped. In 1944 the Allies were flying bombing missions all around Auschwitz anyway. That year, the Jews of Hungary wrote to Western leaders begging them to bomb the railway lines to Auschwitz in order to save the Hungarian Jews. But the Allies chose not to.

THE FINAL STAGES

In April 1943, the final killings within the Warsaw ghetto were taking place and the inmates chose to make a suicidal stand against the Germans. They bought weapons from the partisans and led a running battle for several weeks with the Germans, killing some in the process. In the confusion some people were able to escape via the sewers. The ghetto was wiped out in the same year, 1943. Although the fightback against the Germans was a boost for Jewish morale it probably sped up the destruction of the other ghettos. With the closure of the Polish ghettos the extermination of the Polish Jews was at an end.

BELOW *As the Warsaw ghetto uprising comes to an end, civilians are lined up ready for deportation.*

THE DEATH MARCHES

As World War II played itself out and Germany faced defeat, the decision was taken to leave nothing behind for the advancing Soviet troops to find. The remaining ghettos in Poland and the death camps were emptied in the dead of winter in 1945. Starving people in inadequate clothes were forced to march to camps in Germany where they were to be put to use in the war effort. It was clear that most of them were in no fit state to walk, let alone be of any use when they arrived. Many historians and survivors have suggested that the intention of the Nazis was that they should die en route, and these journeys became known as 'death marches'.

Many prisoners were machine-gunned when they arrived at their destinations. Others were dumped in overcrowded, disease-ridden camps and left for the Allied troops to find. In camps such as Chelmno and Sobibor the remaining Jews were forced to dig up the bodies of the victims and burn them on huge pyres. They had to burn records and pull down the buildings. In some cases trees were planted on the site in order to disguise it.

RIGHT *A typhus sufferer in Belsen camp, one of many left in camps by the Nazis for the Allies to find.*

ABOVE *Summer 1944: Hungarian Jews are deported from Budapest to Auschwitz.*

Negotiating for Jewish lives

In 1944, faced with military losses, Adolf Eichmann, the Nazi leader who organized the deportations to the east, began negotiations with some of the Allies over the survival of the Hungarian Jews. Historians disagree over the significance of the event. Some, such as Martin Gilbert, believe that the Nazis wanted to keep the 600,000 Jews in Hungary under control while they made arrangements to transport them to the gas chambers.

Others, like British Prime Minister of the time, Winston Churchill, saw the negotiations as an effort on the part of the Nazis to split the Allies. They negotiated only with the British and Americans, asking for 10,000 fully supplied trucks to fight the USSR in exchange for freeing a million Jews. Few have considered it a genuine attempt on the part of the Allies to save lives, although that is a possibility.

Should the Allies have seriously tried to negotiate for Jewish lives? If they had supplied the Germans with cash or trucks what would have been the effect on the alliance with the USSR? The negotiations failed and, in May and June 1944, 450,000 Hungarian Jews were transported to Auschwitz.

CHAPTER 5

What were the Consequences of the Holocaust?

AFTERMATH

In the months that followed the end of World War II, the whole of Europe was in ruins. Jewish survivors returned to their homes, some to be murdered in their own neighbourhoods by anti-Semitic groups, most to find their relatives dead. Very quickly the main wartime allies – Britain, the USA and the USSR – began to disagree about how to deal with defeated Germany.

The countries in eastern Europe which had been liberated by the USSR joined a Communist bloc. The countries of western Europe, liberated by the USA and Britain, joined a rival bloc. Germany was divided into two parts between them. The rivalry that developed between the USA and the USSR, the main super-powers of the post-war world, became known as the Cold War.

War crimes trials were held in Nuremberg, Germany in 1945–6 and charges were brought against the leaders of organizations that were responsible for the conduct of the war. Because of the Cold War, both sides wanted influential Germans such as public leaders, industrialists and scientists on their side. The continuation of war crimes trials would have made this difficult. The Cold War began to demand new technology and German scientists, most of whom had worked on behalf of Nazism, had skills that were likely to give one side an advantage.

Many war criminals slipped out of Europe or changed their identities. One such criminal, Klaus Barbie, the head of the Gestapo in Lyons in France, was given help to escape to Bolivia by the US intelligence service, which wanted him to work for it. The initial war crimes trials in Nuremberg found over twenty important Nazi leaders guilty and sentenced some to death, others to long prison terms. Minor trials continued until 1949 and prison sentences were handed out. But after that, the prosecution of war criminals was abandoned.

? EVENT IN QUESTION

The Nuremberg trials: genuine justice or a token?

Did the Nuremberg trials represent genuine justice for the 6 million people who died in the Holocaust? Or were they just a show put on to ease the guilt of Western powers that did nothing to prevent the genocide? Did political events such as the Cold War mean that Nazis escaped because they could be useful to one side or the other?

Trials of Nazis continued in individual countries. The State of Israel pursued Nazi leaders well into the 1980s; for example, they captured Adolf Eichmann in 1960 (see page 47). Yet of the 100,000 or more people who knowingly took part in genocide only some 10,000 ever stood trial. Many of those who did served only very brief prison sentences.

BELOW *Hermann Goering in the witness stand at the Nuremberg trials, 1946. Goering committed suicide before he could be hanged.*

ABOVE *Jews in the Bergen Displaced Persons' Camp (near Belsen, Germany) protest after hearing that the Exodus, a ship carrying about 4,500 Jewish refugees to Palestine, has been boarded and seized (see page 46).*

DISPLACED PERSONS

In 1945 about 200,000 Jews were in concentration camps, mostly in western Europe. In the months following liberation, thousands died from disease and starvation. Others returned home to try to pick up their lives. The majority with nowhere to go remained in Displaced Persons' (DP) camps in Germany and Austria under the control of the British and American occupying troops. Their numbers were swelled by thousands of Jews from eastern Europe.

Some Jewish refugees were allowed to emigrate to the USA but by 1947 there were still about 300,000 Jews in DP camps. Large numbers of them were Zionists who felt there was no

? **WHAT IF...**

the Holocaust had never happened?

If the Holocaust had never happened, would Israel have come into existence? Perhaps it would: the Zionist movement existed before the Holocaust and would have continued to fight for a Jewish state in Palestine. Some questions arise though:

- Would the Zionist movement have been so strong without the 300,000 Jews in DP camps in western Europe?

- Would it have had the support of the American Jewish community?

- The Soviet Union argued at the UN in favour of the creation of a Jewish state. Would it have done so if it hadn't had its own displaced Jews?

- If there hadn't been all those Jewish people with nowhere to go, would the other states with a vote at the UN have agreed to it?

If the answer to some of these questions is 'no', then it is possible that there might never have been an Israeli state.

future for Jews in Europe and wanted a homeland of their own. They saw that homeland as Palestine. In 1947, Palestine was still occupied by Britain. It had a small community of Jews, living alongside a majority of Arabs who wanted to form an independent Arab state.

Meanwhile the US army had the burden of feeding and housing 800,000 displaced persons, 300,000 of whom – the Jews – were becoming increasingly angry about their situation. In 1946 and 1948 there were elections in the USA. President Harry Truman badly needed the support of influential Jews in New York if he was to keep his job.

THE STATE OF ISRAEL

In 1946 Truman proposed to the British that 100,000 Jews be allowed to emigrate to Palestine. Britain, however, did not agree to Truman's suggestion. The US army had a serious problem on its hands: 300,000 distressed, rootless people demanding a homeland. As many as 69,000 displaced Jews began illegal attempts to get into Palestine aboard unseaworthy ships, rousing public sympathy around the world.

BELOW *The* Exodus, *with its Jewish refugees still on board.*

Then, in 1947, Britain decided to hand over the control of Palestine to the United Nations. Britain was no longer a super-power and was reluctant to carry on holding responsibility for Palestine. The United Nations voted to divide Palestine between the Jews and the Arabs. In May 1948 the British left Palestine and the State of Israel was declared. A war followed between Palestinian Arabs and the Jewish settlers. It was narrowly won by the settlers.

For the next twelve years Israel was concerned with its survival as a new state and the Holocaust was put aside as survivors tried to rebuild a normal life. Other countries could celebrate the heroism of their soldiers and civilians in wartime. Yet the Jewish survivors in Israel had very few such examples of bravery to look back at, just years of terrible suffering. Then in 1960 everything changed. A leading Nazi, Adolf Eichmann, was captured by Israeli agents in Argentina and brought to Jerusalem. He went on trial in 1961 and was put to death the following year.

BELOW *Adolf Eichmann behind bullet-proof glass at his trial in Jerusalem.*

❓ EVENT IN QUESTION

The Eichmann trial: justice or justification?

In one way the trial simply meted out justice to war criminal Adolf Eichmann (1906–62), who was responsible for the deaths of millions of people. From another viewpoint it was the beginning of something much bigger: the use of the Holocaust to justify the existence of the State of Israel. The prosecution at the trial of Eichmann said the event was not just about what Eichmann did but about the whole of the Holocaust. In other words, the Jewish people needed a safe haven in Israel because of how they had suffered in Europe.

Israel itself was threatened from all sides by hostile Arab states. Within the country, young Israelis had begun to distance themselves from the Holocaust. Survivors reported being constantly asked why they had not fought back. The Israeli Prime Minister, David Ben-Gurion, talked about the need to show the world that there was a conspiracy to exterminate the Jews.

CHAPTER 6

What does the Holocaust Mean Today?

'SHOAH BUSINESS'

Nearly 60 years after the end of the Holocaust, the number of survivors dwindles as even the youngest grow elderly. Since the trial of Adolf Eichmann in 1961, the Holocaust has become increasingly important in world history. For decades it was put aside and wasn't even known as the Holocaust. But in recent years hundreds of Holocaust memorials have been erected in Europe and the USA.

In many ways the Holocaust has become a symbol of horror as much as a historical event. This can be seen most clearly in the USA where there are hundreds of Holocaust memorials and the Holocaust is part of the curriculum in many schools. Yet very few Americans were involved in any way in the Holocaust. Items of clothing and property from murdered Jews have been put on

BELOW An exhibition on display at Auschwitz death camp, which has become a museum dedicated to the memory of the 1.2 million people who died there.

display in hugely expensive museums dedicated to events that happened on another continent. The people who have erected all these memorials believe that studying the horror of those events can help us to learn how to prevent such terrible things happening again.

In some ways, there is more concern about the Holocaust in the USA than the war in Vietnam in which thousands of Americans died, or the treatment of Native Americans during the nineteenth and twentieth centuries. The Holocaust has become big business in recent years, with multi-million dollar movies as well as expensive museums, which bring in lots of tourist dollars. It has led some historians to remark that 'there is no business like Shoah business'.

ABOVE *Photographs of some of the victims of the Holocaust at Yad Vashem in Israel.*

? EVENT IN QUESTION

The granting of Israeli citizenship to the victims

In 1953 Yad Vashem, the Holocaust memorial centre in Israel, gave Israeli citizenship to all Jewish Holocaust victims who had died. In this way the death of the European Jews was associated with the establishment of the State of Israel. Looked at from this point of view it is a noble idea. In some small way all those deaths are given a meaning if they died so that Israel could exist.

But many of the millions of Jews who died had no intention of living in Palestine and might have been opposed to the idea of a Jewish state in Arab territory. Very few of their surviving families bothered to pay the US$12 for the citizenship certificate that Yad Vashem offered. Yad Vashem has since objected to other Holocaust memorials both in the USA and France. The centre's management only withdrew its objections when Yad Vashem was recognized as the only place with the right to register the names of the victims. Does Israel have the right to claim these dead people as its citizens?

MEMORIALS

The remains of concentration camps and other sites associated with the Holocaust have become places both of pilgrimage and of sightseeing. The huge site of Auschwitz camp has been preserved and part of it has been turned into a museum with reconstructed gas chambers. The original ones were destroyed by the retreating Germans. Display cases show the belongings of victims. Auschwitz has become a symbol of the suffering of the Jews.

RIGHT *This monument dedicated to the victims of the Holocaust is in Warsaw, Poland.*

The ghetto in Warsaw has become the symbol of the great courage of those who fought back against impossible odds. In Warsaw itself the ghetto has disappeared and just one or two relics mark its existence. In Yad Vashem, the reconstruction of Warsaw Ghetto Square is one of the first exhibits that the visitor sees.

In the 1990s, a memorial museum was built in Berlin, Germany. In Hamburg the site of a synagogue that was destroyed by the Nazis is marked by a plaque, as is the square from where the city's Jews were deported. The Imperial War Museum in London, Britain established a permanent exhibition dedicated to the Holocaust in 2000. Half a million people visited in the first eighteen months.

BELOW About 700,000 people each year visit Anne Frank House in Amsterdam, Holland, where the Frank family and their friends hid from the Germans for more than two years from 1942 to 1944.

? EVENT IN QUESTION

Marketing the Holocaust

In the last decade a large number of museums, tourist destinations, films, books, educational materials, badges, posters and the like have arisen in relation to the Holocaust. Norman Finkelstein (see page 55) refers to some of this as 'the Holocaust industry'. The Holocaust has, in one sense, become marketable and some people have noticed that there is a profit to be made from it.

Other examples of the 'Holocaust industry' may be found in a Superman comic-book story (where Superman goes back in time to see Auschwitz) and a Holocaust cookbook published in New York in 1996. A popular Israeli TV quiz programme has teenagers scoring points for answering questions about the death camps.

On the one hand, such things can be seen as just harmless examples of the way in which society acknowledges the enormous significance of the Shoah. From another point of view, they point to the exploitation of the Holocaust to make money.

THE USA AND THE HOLOCAUST

In 1947, a proposed memorial to the victims of the Holocaust, to be set up in Riverside Park in New York, was rejected by both the City Arts Commission and by a Jewish American Committee. The arts committee thought such a monument would be too depressing for a public space and seemed 'to refer to foreign, not American, history'. The Jewish committee thought that it would be a constant reminder to Jews that they are a 'helpless minority whose safety and very lives depend upon the whim of the people among whom they live…'

Since then things have changed a great deal. In the late 1980s, a government committee came to the conclusion that it was indeed important for the USA to remember the Holocaust. As plans began in 1987 for a United States Holocaust Memorial Museum in Washington DC, a member of the government, Max Kampelman said: 'Our decision to build such a museum says something about our commitment to human rights and to the kind of nation we want to be.'

Kampelman's comment suggests that the museum is as much about the USA as it is about an event in Europe which took place 60 years ago.

BELOW *The Holocaust Museum in Manhattan, New York.*

Schindler's List

The very successful film *Schindler's List* (1993) tells the story of Oskar Schindler, who saved the lives of over a thousand Jewish workers from his factory in Cracow, Poland. From one point of view, the film brought the Holocaust to a public who had not until then known much about it. However, the film has also been criticized because of the way the Holocaust is represented in the film. Most of the heroes, in true Hollywood fashion, somehow manage to survive. The villain of the film, the work-camp commander, is shown as a pure madman from whom the audience distances itself. The audience can watch the film and feel that they have nothing in common with such an evil person.

However, as historians have shown, most of the people who carried out the Holocaust were ordinary men and women, in some cases with families. The vast majority of those responsible were definitely not raving maniacs. If, however, we leave the cinema linking the atrocity of the Holocaust with a 'baddie', who is hanged for his evil deeds, does this help us to understand how the Holocaust really took place?

ABOVE *A scene from the movie* Schindler's List. *Oscar Schindler brings Jewish women back from Auschwitz death camp to his factory in Brinnlitz.*

53

RIGHT *On Holocaust Memorial Day in London a survivor displays her camp number tattooed on her arm.*

REPARATIONS

Since the 1950s, Germany has paid out US$93 billion in pensions and compensation for survivors of the Holocaust and to the State of Israel. Some survivors have complained that too much of the money has gone to the Jewish organizations that campaigned for the compensation or has financed museums or research, rather than going to the individuals who emerged from the camps in 1945.

Since the end of the Cold War in 1991, further issues have arisen. At the end of the war thousands of ghetto and death camp survivors remained in eastern Europe. Owing to bad relations with the USSR, no compensation was paid to them. When the

Cold War came to an end, agreements were made with Byelorussia, Ukraine and Russia to compensate survivors with small one-off payments. Yet the survivors in Czechoslovakia, Latvia, Romania and Bulgaria received nothing. Former members of the German SS in these countries, however, receive a war pension from the German government.

In the 1990s the Swiss government and Swiss banks also came under criticism for not making enough effort to trace relatives of survivors to return money from bank accounts. Under enormous pressure, in 1998 the Swiss banks paid out over a billion US dollars in reparations. Further claims have been made against Switzerland for dealing in gold looted by Nazis from Jewish people and confiscating money from the Swiss bank accounts of German Jews. This was done to compensate for the loss of Swiss property caused by the war.

While all the quarrelling goes on, the survivors grow older and frailer and soon there will be few people to receive the compensation. One critic of all this, Norman Finkelstein, has pointed out that the USA also dealt in German gold and took money from German bank accounts in the USA which may have belonged to Jewish people. Such money was confiscated to compensate for American losses during World War II.

BELOW *Norman Finkelstein has expressed strong and controversial views about the way that the memory of the Holocaust has been used by various groups for their own purposes.*

? PEOPLE IN QUESTION

Norman Finkelstein

The American Jewish scholar, Norman Finkelstein (1953–), is the son of Holocaust survivors. His book, *The Holocaust Industry*, published in 2000, suggests why there is such a concern to remember the Holocaust. Organizations such as the Shoah Institute in the USA see the collection of the testimony (stories) of Holocaust survivors as a duty owed to the memory of those who died.

Yet Finkelstein argues that the memory of the Holocaust is used by the State of Israel to justify its harsh and unfair policies towards Palestinians. He says that supporters of the Israeli government's treatment of the Palestinians point to the Holocaust as their reason for strongly defending themselves against anyone that attacks them.

HOLOCAUST DENIAL

In spite of the overwhelming evidence, there are people who deny aspects of the Holocaust or even that it happened at all. Some set out to prove that Hitler had little knowledge of the Holocaust. Some claim that there were no gas chambers or death camps. They say that Jews certainly died but not in the numbers claimed, or that their deaths were an incidental by-product of the war.

They support these claims by pointing out that there is no evidence on paper to show that Hitler ordered the Final Solution and that the real gas chambers at Auschwitz are no longer there. It is claimed that there is no physical evidence that the death camps such as Chelmno and Sobibor ever existed. In its extreme form, Holocaust deniers say that the Holocaust is a Jewish invention designed to justify Israel's position in the Middle East and cover up a plan by Jews to dominate the world.

BELOW *The entrance to Auschwitz death camp. The sign hanging over the gate says 'Work sets you free.'*

? PEOPLE IN QUESTION

David Irving

The best-known figure in Holocaust denial is the writer David Irving (1938–). He wrote a book in which he claimed that Hitler knew nothing of the Holocaust. After a long history of denying the Holocaust, during which he was banned from Austria and condemned by various anti-racist groups, Irving finally reached a mass audience in 2000. He took court action in London against the publisher and author of a book that accused him of denying the Holocaust had happened.

The trial was widely reported in newspapers and the court had to be moved to a bigger room in order to accommodate all the people who wanted to listen. Irving lost the case and the judge called him an 'anti-Semitic, racist, active pro-Nazi who distorts history.' Yet the trial allowed him a huge amount of publicity for his views.

ABOVE *David Irving.*

All Holocaust deniers choose to reinterpret or deny the facts of history for various purposes. Their reasons might be anti-Semitism, opposition to the State of Israel or the belief that the Holocaust was invented to wring cash reparations out of Germany. Perhaps these people are unable to accept that a modern, civilized European country such as Germany could have committed or taken part in such an act.

COULD THERE BE ANOTHER HOLOCAUST?

In 1948 the United Nations Geneva Convention defined genocide as 'acts committed with the intent to destroy, in whole or in part, a national, ethnic, racial or religious group…' Working from such a definition, there have been a number of other genocides. During World War I, some 1.5 million Armenians were systematically killed in Turkey. In the USSR after World War II, millions of people from several distinct ethnic groups were deported to Siberia. A quarter of them died on the way. In Cambodia during the 1970s, around 2 million people died at the hands of their own government.

ABOVE *Ethnic Albanian children hold portraits of relatives murdered by Serb forces in Kosovo during 'ethnic cleansing' in 1999.*

In the 1980s, the Indonesian government killed about one-third of the population of East Timor. In former Yugoslavia during the 1990s, the term 'ethnic cleansing' was used to describe the removal and murder of people because of their cultural identity. Rwanda in 1994 saw the army, presidential guard and extremists from the Hutu militias killing an estimated 200,000–500,000 civilians, most of them from the main minority group in Rwanda, the Tutsis.

There are also examples of societies passing laws that share some characteristics with the Nuremberg Laws of Nazi Germany. South Africa, as well as some southern states of the United States, used to have a series of racist laws that discriminated against racial minorities.

THE SITUATION TODAY

Similarities have also been drawn between the treatment of Jewish people in eastern Europe in 1939 and the situation of the Palestinians today. Palestinians point to the loss of their own land

LEFT *Scotland marks Holocaust Memorial Day. A girl holds a candle in memory of the victims.*

under Israeli rule and to their bad treatment by the State of Israel. Like some of the Jews of post-war Europe, they feel they have a right to their own independent state.

By 2002, extreme right wing organizations with similar beliefs to the Nazis had gained some political power at national level in Austria, Belgium, France, Holland, Denmark, Italy and Portugal. Racist attacks occur throughout Europe and the USA. Remembering and studying the Holocaust and comparing it with other modern acts of genocide is one way of arming future generations of people against the kind of indifference that made it possible.

? EVENT IN QUESTION

*W*as the *H*olocaust unique?

The Holocaust can be viewed as a unique event because of the way it used doctors and nurses, civil servants, lawyers, train drivers, local government officers – mostly ordinary people – to carry out its acts. It can also be seen as unique due to its use of technology to murder on an industrial scale. However, there have been many other acts of genocide both before and after 1939–45. Some of these genocides, like that of the Armenians in Turkey, were also systematic and in this sense the Holocaust was not unique.

Timeline

11th–12th century
Massacres of Jews in the Rhineland.

1095–1291
Crusades by Western Christians against the Muslim powers to try to take over Jerusalem and other places holy to Christians.

1215
European Jews are forced to wear particular clothes to mark them out as Jews.

1290
Jews are expelled from England.

1306
Jews are expelled from France.

1648
Massacres of Jews in Poland and Ukraine.

1800s
Jewish people gain civil rights in France.

1881–2
Pogroms carried out against Jews in Russia and Ukraine.

1889
Birth of Adolf Hitler.

1914–18
Jews take part in First World War on behalf of their countries of birth.

1915
An estimated 1.5 million Armenians die in Turkish genocide.

1917
The Balfour Declaration is made, a British statement of support for a national home for the Jews in Palestine.

1919
The Treaty of Versailles makes Germany pay for losses and damage caused by the First World War.

1920
Hitler becomes leader of the NSDAP or Nazi Party.

1923
Hitler and General Erich Ludendorff stage an uprising in Germany. Hitler is imprisoned and writes his autobiography *Mein Kampf*.

1926
Hitler Youth and other anti-Semitic groups are formed in Germany.

1929–1950s
Forced deportations of ethnic Soviet groups in the USSR result in the deaths of millions of people.

1933
Hitler becomes Chancellor of Germany.

1935
Nuremberg laws remove citizenship and all political rights from German Jews.

1938
Kristallnacht: a wave of terror is unleashed on German Jews.

1939–45
World War II.

1939
Ghettos are established in Polish cities.

1940
Germany invades France, Belgium, Holland, Denmark, Norway and Luxembourg.

1941
Operation Barbarossa, the German invasion of the Soviet Union begins. Nazis invade Greece and Yugoslavia.

1941–45
The systematic murder of Jews throughout Europe.

1941
Gas chambers and gas vans are built and put into operation in Poland.

1942
Wannsee Conference plans the extermination of European Jewry.

1943
Warsaw ghetto uprising.

1944
Camp inmates blow up one of the crematoria at Auschwitz. Majdanek death camp is liberated by Soviet troops.

January 1945
Soviet forces liberate Auschwitz death camp.

October 1945
Nuremberg trials begin.

July 1946
Jews are killed in a pogrom in Kielce, Poland.

1947
Boatloads of Jewish refugees begin to arrive in Palestine.

1948
Britain gives up control of Palestine. The State of Israel is declared.

1961
Adolf Eichmann goes on trial in Jerusalem, Israel.

1975–79
An estimated 2 million people die in Cambodia in genocidal attacks.

1993
The US Holocaust Museum opens in Washington, DC.

1994
The film *Schindler's List* wins seven Oscars in Hollywood.

1994
200,000–500,000 Tutsis killed in Rwanda.

1950–99
Reparations to Jewish and other victims of the Holocaust are paid by the German government.

2000
Holocaust denier David Irving goes to court in London to defend his views.

2000
The Imperial War Museum in London opens a permanent Holocaust exhibition. Jewish Museum opens in Berlin.

Glossary

Allies The countries, such as Britain, France and the USA, that fought Germany, Japan and their allies in the Second World War.

Anti-Semitism Hatred of Jewish people.

Aryan The Nazis used this word to mean a white-skinned European person, not of Jewish, Slav or gypsy descent. Aryans were considered members of the 'master race'.

bloc A group of countries that work together because they have similar political interests.

commandant The commanding officer.

communism The belief that all property should be owned by the government and that each person should be paid according to his or her needs.

concentration camp A large prison and work camp where prisoners were often worked to death but not deliberately murdered as in the death camps.

death camps The camps in Poland where Jews and other minority groups were taken to be murdered.

deportation The process of removing people from their homes and forcing them to go to a death, work or concentration camp.

Einsatzgruppen Special units of the SS that operated in the Soviet Union carrying out mass murders of Jews, communists, state officials and partisans.

euthanasia The killing by the Nazis of people they believed were of no use to society, such as disabled people.

Final Solution The Nazi policy of murdering all of Europe's Jews.

gas chamber A room that is filled with poisonous gas in order to kill people.

genocide The deliberate destruction of a group of people on account of their race, religion or beliefs.

Gestapo The German secret police.

ghetto A walled-off area of a town or city where a certain group of people are forced to live.

National Socialists, or Nazi Party Hitler's political party. Its members believed in the rule of one powerful leader and discriminated against people from different countries and cultures. The Nazis used force to conquer other countries.

occupied Europe The parts of Europe occupied by the Nazis during the Second World War.

Palestine A region of the Middle East occupied in 1918 by Britain. Part of it was declared the State of Israel in 1948.

partisan Someone who fights for a particular cause. The term was used in the Second World War to describe small groups of people who operated secretly against the Nazi occupiers in their country.

pogrom An organized massacre of civilians.

reparations Money that is paid by a country that has lost a war in return for the harm it has done.

Shoah The Hebrew name for the murder of the Jews by the Nazis.

Slav A member of a group of peoples in central and eastern Europe, including Russians, Poles, Czechs and Bulgarians.

SS (*Schutzstaffen*) Protection squads. Originally Hitler's bodyguards, they later organized and ran the death camps.

underground resistance The movement that fought the Nazi forces occupying Europe. It attacked the Nazis, gave information to the Allies and in some cases helped Jews and prisoners of war to escape.

United Nations An association of many countries formed after the Second World War to try to solve political problems and improve people's living conditions.

USSR Union of Soviet Socialist Republics.

work camp A camp where prisoners had to work for the Nazi war effort.

Zionism The Jewish nationalist movement. It aimed to create a Jewish state in Palestine.

Further information

BOOKS

Martin Gilbert *Never Again: a History of the Holocaust* (Harper Collins, 2000)

R. G. Grant *New Perspectives: The Holocaust* (Hodder Wayland, 1997)

Thomas Kenneally *Schindler's Ark* (Hodder and Stoughton, 1975)

Pat Levy *The Holocaust: Causes* (Hodder Children's Books, 2000)

Pat Levy *The Holocaust: Survival and Resistance* (Hodder Children's Books, 2000)

Sean Sheehan *The Holocaust: After the Holocaust* (Hodder Children's Books, 2000)

Sean Sheehan *The Holocaust: The Death Camps* (Hodder Children's Books, 2000)

SOURCES

Yehuda Bauer *Rethinking the Holocaust* (Yale University Press, 2001)

Dan Cohn Sherbok *Understanding the Holocaust* (Cassell, 1999)

Tim Cole *Images of the Holocaust: The Myth of the 'Shoah Business'* (Duckworth, 1999)

Lucy Dawidowicz *The War against the Jews 1933–45* (Penguin, 1975)

Norman G. Finkelstein *The Holocaust Industry: Reflections on the Exploitation of Jewish Suffering* (Verso, 2000)

Roberto Finzi *Anti-Semitism From its European Roots to the Holocaust* (The Windrush Press, 1999)

Robert Gelately *Backing Hitler* (Oxford University Press, 2001)

Daniel Goldhagen *Hitler's Willing Executioners* (Abacus, 1996)

Michael Marrus *The Holocaust in History* (Penguin, 1987)

Ed. Ruby Rohrlich *Resisting the Holocaust* (Berg, 1998)

Ed Kate Taylor *Holocaust Denial* (Searchlight Educational Trust, 2000)

NOTE ON SOURCES

There is an enormous amount of material relating to the Holocaust but it is important to find out what is genuinely informative and what is misinformation or propaganda.

When looking at a source you should ask yourself:

1. Who wrote it? Survivors from Auschwitz as well as the Nazi commandant of the camp have written accounts of what they experienced and their very different viewpoints have to be taken into account.

2. Why did they write it? A historian might have a particular idea to get over and might select events or distort the account to prove a point. The work of David Irving is a clear example of this.

3. When did they write it? Can we trust accounts of the Holocaust written fifty or more years after the event? Some accounts by 'survivors' were later shown to have been invented by the author.

4. Is it really source material? The film *Schindler's List* is based on real events but some of what you see is fictional.

Index